THE DEEP SILENCE
OF MY PEACE

Reference Notes

The source for this pamphlet is Recording #8A-2,
a Joel Goldsmith class from the
1952 New Washington Series: Tape 5, side 2.
This recording is currently available in audiotape,
CD, or MP3 format at www.joelgoldsmith.com.

Other Titles in This Series

THE DEEP SILENCE
OF MY PEACE

Joel S. Goldsmith

Acropolis Books, Publisher
Longboat Key, Florida

The Deep Silence of My Peace by Joel S. Goldsmith

From Chapter 15 of Collected Essays of Joel S. Goldsmith,
© 1986 Thelma McDonald.

Acropolis Books, Inc.
Longboat Key, Florida
www.joelgoldsmithbooks.com

Except the Lord build the house,
they labour in vain that build it.

Psalm 127

Illumination dissolves all material ties and binds men together with the golden chains of spiritual understanding; it acknowledges only the leadership of the Christ; it has no ritual or rule but the divine, impersonal universal Love; no other worship than the inner Flame that is ever lit at the shrine of Spirit. This union is the free state of spiritual brotherhood. The only restraint is the discipline of Soul; therefore, we know liberty without license; we are a united universe without physical limits; a divine service to God without ceremony or creed. The illumined walk without fear – by Grace.

The Infinite Way

THE DEEP SILENCE
OF MY PEACE

"My peace I give unto you: not as the world giveth, give I unto you"—but *My* peace, a peace to which you must cling even when the turmoil which disturbs the outer world comes into your world to bring about either doubt or fear of those things or conditions that exist in the world.

If you really want to attain a sense of peace, learn to drop all thought or concern for whatever it is that is disturbing in the outer picture. Now, it is not easy for me to write this any more than it is easy for you to read it, but the desire in the hearts of most of us right now is for some solution to an outer problem, a problem of human existence, to something that is disturbing us in the world of health or wealth. Most of us are concerned about something in our human affairs and are seeking a solution. There is nothing wrong with that; the solution must appear because harmony must appear, but we will fail to find the solution as long as we are concerned with the problem and the solution to the problem. We can have the answer to that problem here and now if we can sufficiently drop our concern for it in the realization of this "*My* peace," that is, the Christ-peace. This is Jesus speaking:

"My peace I give unto you: not as the world giveth"—not the peace of physical health or material wealth, not the satisfaction of personal desires, but something far transcending these, something that, when we experience it, wipes out entirely the need

for human demonstration. That is what we want to achieve here and now. Right now, we must, and many of us can drop this concern, lose concern for whatever it is, whatever the nature of it may be, that we brought with us when we turned to these words. We cannot do this humanly by telling it to get out or "get... behind me, Satan," but we can open our consciousness at this minute to a realization of "My peace."

Watch this as it flows through your consciousness; watch as you open yourself, even with the question: "What is this 'My peace'? What is the spiritual nature of peace? What is the spiritual nature of harmony?" You will remember that to be that man whose being is in Christ, we must come to the end of the road of seeking and searching and come to some measure of awareness that we have already arrived. To do that, we relax from every sense of desire for achievement or desire for demonstration in the feeling that the presence of God dissolves all false appearances.

The presence of God is a "peace, be still" to every type of storm. There are more storms than ever were on the seas; there are more storms in our thought than on all the oceans, but the Christ is a "peace, be still" to every kind of storm, to every form of discord, to every nature of inharmony. "Peace, be still ... My peace"—*My* peace, the Christ-peace, "the peace that passeth understanding," is the peace that comes with the realization:

"I will never leave thee, nor forsake thee." If you walk through the water, I will be with you. "Whither thou goest, I will go ... thy people shall be my people." Never—"I will never leave thee, nor forsake thee." Whithersoever thou goest, I will go. Yea, though you walk through the valley of the shadow of death, I

will walk with you. I will be with you, I will be in you, and I will be through you. Fear not, fear not, I am with you.

From the depth of this inner silence come forth the healing waters. These waters bring everlasting life. Out of the depth of this silence comes the Spirit, which appears as our cloud by day and our pillar of fire by night. Out of the depth of this silence comes the safety and the security, which always follow the peace that God gives.

The reason for peace is that there is nothing to fear. While there is something to fear, there is no peace. Once the peace has descended upon us, the prayer is complete; the reason for disturbance, sickness, and lack has gone. The feeling of peace is the successful prayer. There is no successful communion until "the peace that passeth understanding" descends upon us.

All prayer, all communion with God, is only for one purpose—not to make any kind of demonstration, but to achieve for us this sense of peace, or well-being, this realization: "Lo, I am with you until the end of time. Lo, I am always with you." Let us have that sense of the divine Presence, and we shall have the answered prayer. Let us fail to achieve this sense of peace, and the prayer is not a prayer. In "*My* presence," the fire does not burn, the water does not drown; in "*My* presence," the storms do not rage. The power of Christ is the answer to every form of inharmony. The feeling of the Presence is in itself a prayer. Let us understand this: Our problem is at an end, not when we think we have found a solution, but when we have felt this inner peace.

There is a bond between all of us, the bond that holds us together at this moment. That bond is the love of God. That love of God is our mutual at-one-ment. It makes us at one with God and at- one with each other so that the flow of God to and through any one of us is instantaneously the flow of God through everyone within range of our being. "One with God is a majority," and because we are one with God and one with each other, all that the Father has is showing forth, is manifesting as our individual experience, the individual experience of each one of us. Whatever is true spiritually of one of us in demonstration is now true of all of us because of our oneness with each other through our oneness in God; so the "peace, be still" that is of God, that touches the Soul of one of us, touches the Soul of all of us.

The solution to the outer problem is automatically taken care of in the realization of this inner peace. The peace within produces harmony and joy without. The activity of

Christ within results in the stilling of the waves without. The "peace, be still" within appears as the daily manna without. The realization of this divine Presence, this feeling of divine Love through us, is the temple of God in which we live and move and have our being—even when we are out in the world. The word of God is our abiding place. Even when we move in and out of this world, we are abiding in this Word if we feel this divine Presence.

I will never leave you, nor forsake you, but you must abide in Me; you must abide in My word. I will never leave you, nor forsake you. I will be with you, whithersoever thou goest, but you must turn within to Me; you must make Me your abiding place; you must take My word into your mouth, into your consciousness. You must take the remembrance of My presence with you wherever you go. I will never leave you nor forsake you, but be sure that you do not leave the Word out of your mouth.

Recognize the divine Presence in the heart and soul of all those you meet, friend or foe. Recognize that the individual soul is the abiding place of God. That the world itself does not know it is of no concern to you or me. They, too, will awaken as we recognize God in the midst of them.

In this work that we are doing now, I want to reveal to you a principle of healing, of protecting, and of supplying, but a principle that will operate without your taking thought, without your making statements, without your doing mental work, and without your begging or pleading or beseeching God. I would like to show you a principle of healing that operates completely without what the metaphysical world calls treatment. In this teaching, you will find that the healing principle is a state of peace that we achieve through the realization of the Presence. That is our form of prayer—just the realization of the Presence, just the feeling of a state of peace.

We remain in communion until a sense of peace steals over us, a sense of peace which comes from but one recognition:

I am with you; I will never leave you nor forsake you. I, in the midst of you, am mighty. "My presence will go before you to make the crooked places straight." "I will go before you to prepare a place for you." "My peace I give unto you: not as the world giveth"—not with human honors or human wealth, but a peace transcending man's understanding, a peace that comes when the Christ is enthroned in your consciousness as the source of your health and the source of your supply.

No other peace can be lasting, except the peace that comes as the Christ is enthroned as the source of good and as the only power in individual experience.

"I live; yet not I, but Christ liveth my life.... I can do all things through Christ." Christ is my strength; Christ is my redeemer, my savior; Christ is the law of resurrection unto my body and unto my business; Christ is my bread and wine and water— not to be achieved, not to be earned. Christ never leaves me nor forsakes me. Therefore, the bread and the water and the wine and the meat are always here within my being: I am with you, and I am the bread of life. I am with you, and I am the meat. I am with you, and I am the wine, and I am the water, and I am the resurrection. I am life eternal, and I, Life eternal, will never leave you nor forsake you. My peace I give unto you.

No longer will you live by bread but by My presence. My presence will be sufficient for you. You will no longer seek anything except for Me, and you will know that in finding Me, the Christ, you will have found your peace, security, confidence, reward, health, strength, and eternality. No longer seek after the things of the world; otherwise, you cannot receive the peace that the world knows nothing of. Seeking the things of the world, you find the peace that the world can give you. Seeking the realization of My presence, you will find "the peace that passeth understanding."

In this prayer, the nature of the problem is of no importance—only the realization of this peace, of this Presence. It will take care of the problem regardless of its nature or its intensity or of the length of its duration. "Though your sins be as scarlet, they shall be as white as snow"—in one instant.

I will take you by a way; I will take you by a way called the Christ, in which every thought, every need, and every desire will be satisfied and fulfilled in the realization of the Word; Christ is my fulfillment; Christ is my savior; Christ is the source and fount of all my good. I shall look unto Christ, not unto man, but unto Christ, unto this sense of peace within me. In the realization of this peace, I have found the Christ; I have realized the Christ. The Christ has become visible and tangible.

Sometimes, in this meditation, I see a luminous crucifix right before my closed eyes, and it symbolizes the crucifying of our faith, belief, and dependence on anything external to our own being. Right now, we are crucifying our faith or dependence on a presence or power outside of our own being. As we rise above the crucifying of our outer dependence, we make the ascension into a state of consciousness in which, regardless of the storm, we close the eyes and say: "'Peace, be still.' My peace is with me."

Think now—that from the moment you have crucified your faith and dependence, your reliance on man and things, and have come into the realization that a state of peace within is life eternal and harmonious without; from that moment, you have made the ascension from this world. And only then can you say with the Master:

"'I have overcome the world.' I have overcome the need for anything or anyone. I have found Christ within to be my salvation, my supplier and my supply, my healer, and my redeemer. I have found that the source of satisfaction is this realization of peace within. My fulfillment now is always from within. I have crossed out the belief that my help must come from without. I have crossed out the belief that anything or anyone external is necessary

in the realization of my eternal harmony." All that has come about through the feeling of peace within, not due to anything without, but due to a divine Presence within. The divine Presence has always been there. Now, when the storms threaten without and the waves dash against our ship, let us remember this experience.

It may take five minutes for the peace to descend; it may take fifteen minutes. There are obstinate beliefs in this world, but if we are patient and know what it is we are waiting for—the assurance from within—it will descend. That is all we are waiting for— the assurance from within. The prayer is not complete until the assurance comes from within: "Lo, I am with you alway ... Fear not, I am with you."

How easy it is to rest in the deep Silence, to relax all cares. "Ah, yes," you say, "but when we return to the world, aren't the troubles still there?" No, not for you and not for me. A thousand may feel them at your left and ten thousand at your right, but they will not come nigh you as you dwell in this deep Silence.

It may take practice, but whenever agitation comes to your thought, find a place to rest, relax, and wait for this peace to descend upon you. As this peace descends upon you inwardly, you may be sure, whatever the name or nature of the storm without, it also is being stilled.

Isn't it easy in this atmosphere to say, "Father, forgive them; they know not what they do"? All these disturbers of the world—isn't it easy to forgive them and to realize that they have disturbed only because of their ignorance of this peace, just as we were ignorant of it before we started this communion? Nothing that defileth or maketh a lie can enter the deep Silence. By this, you can see that we are not disturbed by our own fears, doubts, or problems. When we come into a sense of agitation, it is usually because we are disturbed by the world's fears, doubts, and problems. We are merely receiving stations for the world's troubles. If they were our troubles, they would still be troubling us. They never were our troubles, even when they reflected themselves in our affairs.

Those of you who feel this, who are touched by the divine Presence, will want to maintain it always. There is a way: It is the way of frequent silence and frequent meditation, frequent opening of thought to the Christ, to the realization of the divine Presence. At the first flurry of an entrance of the world into your consciousness, retire into this—even while at your work. "Be not afraid; it is I."

As a person, you no longer need to desire anything to want anything or to acknowledge a need for anything. As a person, now, you can relax and be assured that there is a Presence in the midst of you, a Light, a Being, and Its function is to fulfill your entire experience, to fill it full of spiritual good. Its function in the midst of you is to know what things you need and to provide them. There is no need for you to acknowledge any lack. There is no need for you to acknowledge any need. The stillness, the silence, is God's abiding place. In the stillness and in the silence, God lives, expresses, fulfills, reveals, and unfolds, and Its world appears to you in forms of harmony, grace, and beauty.

If you are as a little child, if you are relaxed, if you have given up the personal sense of "I" at this moment—if only for this moment— you come to the place where it is almost as if you were looking over your own shoulder and watching God appear, just as you might watch a sunset or a moonrise and yet not reach out and try to help, quietly be a beholder. Sometimes, when you see a beautiful flower, the first thought that comes into your mind is, "And a fool hath said in his heart there is no God." Have you ever looked at a beautiful flower or a mountain scene, sunrise or sunset, and that thought flashed into your mind, "And a fool hath said in his heart there is no God"? That is because you knew that "only God can make a tree," as the poet has told us. You knew that only God could fashion such a sunset, and create such a mountain setting. You knew it was your joy, pleasure, and privilege to behold God revealing Itself in these beautiful forms and colors. That is all you were doing; you were beholding God revealing Itself to you in these wondrous varieties of beauty and grace.

So in this moment of relaxed Selfhood, in this silent communion, you know now that you can of your own self do nothing; it truly is the Father within you that doeth the works. In this moment of supreme stillness and silence, the human mind is not trying to make a demonstration; the human mind has gone even a step further and acknowledges no lack, no limitation, no need, but feels:

I am home in Thee. "I and my Father are one." I rest in Thee. I feel "the peace that passeth understanding." I know the glow of the divine Presence. He that fashioned me shall preserve me. He shall be a light unto my feet; He shall go to prepare a place for me because His is the kingdom and the power and the glory. This is His kingdom, not mine. This is His power, not mine. This is His glory, not mine. As if we, of our own understanding or power, have raised up this man! No, the

God of Abraham, the God of Isaac, the God of Jacob hath done this thing. And if the Spirit of God dwells in us, that same Spirit that raised up Jesus from the dead will quicken also our mortal bodies.

How can you know if the Spirit of God dwells in you? If you can be relaxed, if you can be at peace, if you can rest, rest. "In quietness and in confidence shall be your strength," not in mental work or treatment. "In quietness and in confidence shall be your strength."

Be still, and let me show you the Father's glory; let me show you how the Father can come to you, revealing health, revealing harmony, revealing peace—and all without your doing a thing. "Not by might, nor by power, but by my spirit, saith the Lord." I will not leave you comfortless. I will send you a comforter—even the Spirit of Truth. And It will be all things to you. Rest from your mental labors, rest from your doubts and from your fears.

No one ever fears who has tasted or touched God. "Yea, though I walk through the valley of the shadow of death," I will not fear. How could David fear, since he had already learned that "Thou art with me"? If, in this moment of stillness and of silence, you feel even the tiniest touch of the Christ, you will never again fear, though you walk through the desert or the wilderness or the waters or the flames or the valley of the shadow of death. You will never again fear because the remembrance of this little touch will be a reassurance:

Before Abraham was, I was right there with you. Lo, I am with you unto the end of the world; I will never leave you nor forsake you. As I was with Abraham, so I will be with you. As I was with Moses in the Red Sea, in the wilderness, so I will be with you. Though the waters pass over you, they will not drown you. I do not ask you to believe the signs. I do not ask you to believe, even if you experience a healing; I will only ask you to believe if you feel the touch within you, the Presence, the Light, the Life.

Remember, if your thoughts want to wander, that it is in quietness and confidence that you find your peace, not in your mental wanderings, not in trying to fulfill some human need—but in quietness and confidence.

When the Master says to us: "Ye shall know the truth, and the truth shall make you free," remember that the truth that you are to know is that "I in the midst of thee am mighty," that *My* peace is your salvation, that quietness and confidence is the prayer, that we do not attain our good by might or by power, but by a gentle Spirit. We are quiet as we accept

God's grace. We let God's grace flow to us, through us, but remember: "Go and tell no man." Tell no one what things you have discovered; do not throw your pearls before the unprepared thought. These things that are whispered to you in silence will be shouted from the housetops as demonstration, not by your voice, not by rushing to tell your friend or neighbor, but by demonstration.

Be still, be still and know. But be still and know; do not do it aloud. "Be still and know."

Made in United States
Orlando, FL
21 February 2024